Good Nigh., ...
Classroom Questions

A SCENE BY SCENE TEACHING GUIDE

Amy Farrell

SCENE BY SCENE
ENNISKERRY, IRELAND

Scene by Scene
11 Millfield, Enniskerry
Wicklow, Ireland.
www.scenebysceneguides.com

Good Night, Mr. Tom Classroom Questions byAmy Farrell. —1st ed.
ISBN 978-1-910949-17-7

Contents

Chapter One

1.   Why are children being sent to live with strangers as the story begins?

2.   Describe Willie's appearance.

3.   Describe Tom's appearance.

4.   Is Tom a kind man? Explain your answer.

5.   What sort of woman is Willie's mother, based on what we have read so far?

6.   What sort of life has Willie had up to now, do you think? Explain your answer, using examples from the story.

7.   Why does Willie faint? What does this tell you about him?

8.   What do we find out about Tom's family?

9.   Is Tom feeling confident about looking after Willie? Explain your answer.

Chapter Two

1. Describe Sammy, Tom's dog.

2. Why do you think Willie offers to carry Tom's bag for him?

3. What does Mrs. Fletcher tell Tom about other children that have come to stay in the area?

4. What sort of woman is Mrs. Fletcher, in your opinion? Use examples from the story to back up your points.

5. Describe the surroundings where Tom lives.

6. Why is Willie so amazed to see Ivor milking a cow?

7. Why must the villagers black out their windows at night?

8. Are you surprised by anything in Mrs. Beech's letter?

9. "Willie's arms and legs were covered in bruises, weals and sores." How would you feel if you were Tom?

10. "Willie had never eaten cake before". What does this tell you about Willie's life in London?

11. Describe Willie's attic room.

12.   Why does Willie start crying at bed-time?

Chapter Three

1. Why does Willie wake up in the middle of the night?

2. "He didn't want everyone to see the marks of his sins."
   What does Willie mean by this?
   Where do you think he came up with this idea?

3. What does Doctor Little say about Willie?

4. Are the villagers friendly and welcoming to Willie?
   Explain your answer using examples from the story.

5. How do you know this story is set during wartime?

Chapter Four

1. Why does it take Willie so long to choose a sweet in the newsagent's?

2. "He felt a mixture of astonishment at himself and irritation that his rigid daily routine was going to be broken after forty undisturbed years." Explain how Tom is feeling after he offers to read the comic to Willie.

3. Why doesn't Willie go into the toy shop?

4. Why does Tom's heart sink when Willie notices the paint shop?

5. Why is the librarian so surprised to see Tom and Willie together in the library?

6. Why is Tom having doubts about having Willie to stay with him?

7. Is Miss Thorne, the librarian, right to feel sorry for Willie "away from his loving home and now dumped with an irritable old man"?

Chapter Five

1. Does Tom mind that Willie has wet the bed again?

2. What different things surprise Willie in the church?

3. What does the Prime Minister, Mr. Chamberlain, announce on the wireless (radio)?

4. What does Mr. Chamberlain say they will be fighting against?

5. According to Willie's mother, what was Sunday for?

6. Why had Willie never played with his classmates? How do you feel about this?

7. What job do they begin in Willie's garden?

Chapter Six

1. What is Zach like? Explain your answer.

2. Is Zach nice to Willie? Explain your answer.

3. Why does Tom usually avoid meetings and social activities?

4. Why does Zach change Willie's name?

5. Why is Willie afraid to have a bath?
    What is your reaction to this?

Chapter Seven

1. Why is Willie so disappointed when he races Sam to the gate?

2. What does Zach notice about Willie's appearance?

3. Why is George reluctant to ask Willie to go blackberry picking?

4. Why doesn't Willie talk much as he picks blackberries with the other children?

5. Does the day go well for Willie? Explain.

6. If you were Willie, would you be glad to spend time with Zach and the others? Explain your opinion.

Chapter Eight

1.   Why is Willie so anxious when Mrs. Hartridge speaks
        to him?

2.   How does he feel about being in Mrs. Black's class?
        Why does he feel this way?

3.   Do you think Tom is understanding and helpful when
        Willie comes home from school after his first day?

4.   What does Tom realise about Willie when he helps him
        to write his name?

5.   How has life changed for Tom since Willie has come
        to stay?

Chapter Nine

1. Why was Tom disappointed when the postman arrived?

2. What nice things does Tom do for Willie because it's his birthday?

3. Which presents does Willie especially like?

4. Why does Willie lose track of time in the church?

5. Does Willie have a good birthday? Explain your answer.

Chapter Ten

1.   Why have some of the evacuees left Little Weirwold?

2.   How do you know Zach is waiting for someone to arrive?

3.   Why has Willie never seen a show in a theatre or gone to the cinema?

4.   Do you notice anything different about how Willie acts with his friends in this chapter?

5.   What different types of games do the children talk about playing?

6.   Why are Willie and Zach such good friends, in your opinion?

7.   Why is Willie worried about having his friends in his bedroom?

8.   Is Tom an understanding man? Use examples from this chapter to help explain your answer.

Chapter Eleven

1. What news was in the letter from Willie's mother?

2. What changes has Tom noticed in Willie since he came to stay with him?

3. What changes does Mrs. Fletcher notice in Tom?

4. What do the other children think of Willie's bedroom?

5. What does George think about school?

6. What information does Carrie give us about inequality between girls and boys in Little Weirwold?

7. Why can't Zach act in the Nativity play?

8. What is different when Willie wakes up the day after his friends visit? Do you think this means anything?

Chapter Twelve

1. Has life in the village been affected by the war?
   Explain your answer.

2. Does Miss Thorne enjoy working on the play with the
   children?

3. How does Willie impress everyone when they're
   practising their lines?

4. Why is Tom so pale when Willie comes home?

Chapter Thirteen

1. What is Willie doing as the chapter begins?

2. What instructions does Tom give the choir?

3. Do Willie and Tom have a good relationship?
Explain your opinion, using examples from this chapter.

Chapter Fourteen

1.   What's wrong with Lucy as the chapter begins?

2.   Why is George "looking very pale and swollen-eyed and wearing a black armband"?

3.   "Willie had tried to cover his embarrassment by scowling". Does Willie remind you of anyone else here? What do you think of this?

4.   What does Carrie speak to Mrs. Hartridge about?

5.   Does Willie's first day in Mrs. Hartridge's class go well for him? Explain your point of view.

6.   Why was Friday going to be a special day for the children?

7.   What will Carrie have to do if she doesn't get a scholarship?

8.   What news does Tom give Willie at the end of the chapter? What is your reaction to this?

Chapter Fifteen

1. Why don't Willie and Tom chat during the journey?

2. Why does Willie have to go?

3. What advice does Tom give Willie about seeing his mother again?

4. How does the young soldier on the train treat Willie?

5. Why does Willie have to see the ticket man when he arrives in London?

6. Why is seeing Willie a "great shock" to his mother?

7. Describe Willie's mother's appearance when he meets her at the station.

8. Is his mother glad to see him, in your opinion?

9. How does she react when Willie smiles at her? What is your response to this?

10. How does Willie's mother treat him when they stop for tea?

11. Is Willie glad to see his mother again? Explain your answer.

12. What "game" does Willie's mother tell him to play when they return home? What is going on here?

13. What "surprise" is waiting at home? What is your reaction to this?

14. How does Willie's mother react to the presents he has brought her from the country?

15. How does Willie's mother react to his drawings? How does this make you feel?

16. "Something heavy hit him across the head and he sank into a cold darkness."
    What is happening here? Why is his mother doing this?

17. Where does Willie wake up?

18. How do you feel at the end of this chapter?

Chapter Sixteen

1. What is life like for Tom, without William?

2. Why does Tom begin to worry about William?

3. Why does Tom visit Mrs. Fletcher?

4. What makes it difficult for Tom to find Deptford?

5. Why is the warden in the air raid shelter so surprised by what Tom has to say?

6. What does Sammy do when they reach the Beech's house?

7. What is the first thing everyone notices when the door is broken down?

8. How do you feel at the end of this chapter?

Chapter Seventeen

1. What state is William in when they discover him?

2. What has happened to the baby?

3. What makes Will realise there's something wrong with the baby?

4. What happens when they reach the hospital?

5. What do the wardens think will happen to Will now?

6. Why did Will have to see a psychiatrist, according to the nurse?

7. Describe Will's appearance when Tom sees him in the hospital.

8. Why can't Tom stay longer with Will?

9. What is your opinion of Mr. Stelton?

10. Do you think that it is right that Will should be sent away to a home?

11. "Tom whipped back the sheets, lifted Will out and wrapped the blanket he was carrying around him."
    Is Tom doing the right thing here, in your opinion?

12.   Is it a difficult journey home to Little Weirwold? Explain your answer.

13.   Do the Littles think Tom was right to kidnap Will?

Chapter Eighteen

1. What does Will dream about?

2. How would you describe Will's health at this stage?

3. How would you describe the care and attention that Tom gives Will at this stage?

4. What different views do Zach and Will have on where babies come from? Are you surprised by this?

5. Why does Will think that Trudy dying was his fault?

6. Why were there soldiers in Little Weirwold?

7. Does Will's visit with Mrs. Hartridge do him good, in your opinion?

Chapter Nineteen

1. What are Zach, Tom and Will doing as this chapter begins?

2. Why did Will and Zach clutch "their stomachs and laugh hysterically"?

3. What sort of village do they arrive in?

4. "He had imagined that the sea would terrify and engulf him." How does Will feel when he sees the sea?

5. Why is Will "overwhelmingly happy at the thought of spending a fortnight in Salmouth"?

6. Zach "had spent several summers by the sea" with his parents. What makes it special this time?

7. Why does Mrs. Clarence's cottage make a great impression on her guests?

8. "Mrs. Clarence didn't understand the relationship of the two boys to Tom."
    What can she not figure out?

9. What damage has the war done in London?

10. Do they enjoy their holiday, in your opinion?

11.   Why is Zach anxious about his parents in this chapter?

12.   What news does Carrie have?

Chapter Twenty

1. What did the children decide to do?

2. Does Will seem afraid? Explain your answer.

3. Describe the man they meet in the cottage.

4. How has this man been upset and affected by the war?

5. Does the artist think Will is talented?
   What does he say about his drawing?

6. What news does Will expect when he sees the policeman, lady and warden?

7. What news do they give him?

8. Are you shocked by this news?

9. Does Will agree when they say Mister Tom kidnapped him?

10. How does Will react when he's asked to go to his room so they can make a decision?

11. How has Will changed since the start of the story?

12. What will happen next for Will?

13.   How do Tom and Will react to this news?

Chapter Twenty One

1.   Describe Carrie's uniform.

2.   Why is Zach worried?

3.   Why must Zach return to London?

4.   How does Will celebrate his birthday?

5.   What nightmare does Will have?
      Why does he have this dream, in your opinion?

6.   What has been happening in London?

7.   What does Will realise in the Littles' house?

Chapter Twenty Two

1. How well is Will coping?

2. How does Will feel about life now?

3. What embarrasses Carrie in school?

4. Why is Carrie feeling lonely?

5. Why does Geoffrey smoke his friend's pipe?

6. Why can't Will concentrate on his drawing?

7. What advice does Geoffrey give Will, to help him deal with his loss? Is this good advice, in your opinion?

8. Why does Will attack the tree?

9. "…he felt overwhelmed with happiness, the tears ran silently down his face."
    What has caused Tom to feel this way?

10. Why does Will want Zach's bike, in your opinion?

11. What good news did Annie Hartridge receive?

12. "Tom was terribly proud of him but then he had been for a long time." How do you feel at this point in the story?

Chapter Twenty Three

1. Why won't Carrie's mother let her wear shorts?
   What do you think about this?

2. What did Will get for Carrie?

3. How is Ginnie different to Carrie?

4. Why is school getting better for Carrie now?

5. Does this story have a happy ending? Explain.

Scene by Scene Series

Good Night, Mr. Tom Classroom Questions

Martyn Pig Classroom Questions

Of Mice and Men Classroom Questions

Pride and Prejudice Classroom Questions

Private Peaceful Classroom Questions

The Fault in Our Stars Classroom Questions

The Old Man and the Sea Classroom Questions

The Outsiders Classroom Questions

To Kill a Mockingbird Classroom Questions

The Spinning Heart Classroom Questions

Visit www.scenebysceneguides.com to find out more about Scene by Scene Classroom Questions teaching guides and workbooks.

Lightning Source UK Ltd.
Milton Keynes UK
UKOW06f1440121015

260355UK00001B/8/P